ANIMAL ALLIES

RAVENS AND WOLVES
TEAM UP!

BY STEPHANIE PETERS

CAPSTONE PRESS
a capstone imprint

Published by Capstone Press, an imprint of Capstone.
1710 Roe Crest Drive, North Mankato, Minnesota 56003
capstonepub.com

Library of Congress Cataloging-in-Publication Data
Names: Peters, Stephanie True, 1965- author.
Title: Ravens and wolves team up! / by Stephanie Peters.
Description: North Mankato, Minnesota : Capstone Press, [2023] | Series: Animal allies | Includes bibliographical references and index. | Audience: Ages 8 to 11 | Audience: Grades 4-6 | Summary: " Ravens and wolves team up for a hunt in this action-packed nonfiction book for young research writers and wildlife fans. One watchful raven + one ravenous wolf = a dangerous duo! In this book, discover how two vastly different animal species team up for a successful hunt. With bird's-eye views, ravens easily spot prey from afar, but these high-flying scavengers need help catching it. Cue the wolves! When alerted by their feathered friends, wolves chase down the prey with lightning-quick speed and big-time teeth. And when they do, this dream team feasts! With in-the-field photographs, fast facts, and bonus back matter, Ravens and Wolves Team Up! will have young research writers and wildlife fans rooting for these Animal Allies"-- Provided by publisher.
Identifiers: LCCN 2022052978 (print) | LCCN 2022052979 (ebook) | ISBN 9781669048725 (hardcover) | ISBN 9781669048671 (paperback) | ISBN 9781669048688 (ebook PDF) | ISBN 9781669048701 (kindle edition) | ISBN 9781669048718 (epub)
Subjects: LCSH: Ravens--Behavior--Juvenile literature. | Wolves--Behavior--Juvenile literature. | Mutualism (Biology)--Juvenile literature.
Classification: LCC QL696.P2367 P46 2023 (print) | LCC QL696.P2367 (ebook) | DDC 598.8/64--dc23/eng/20230105
LC record available at https://lccn.loc.gov/2022052978
LC ebook record available at https://lccn.loc.gov/2022052979

Editorial Credits
Editor: Donald Lemke; Designer: Sarah Bennett; Media Researcher: Svetlana Zhurkin; Production Specialist: Katy LaVigne

Image Credits
Alamy: Gabbro, 11, Peter Llewellyn RF, 25; Getty Images: Corbis/Hulton-Deutsch Collection, 24, GarysFRP, 8, Gerald Corsi, 18, John Morrison, 23, juergen2008, 5, milehightraveler, 27, Stan Tekiela, 4, 19; National Park Service: Doug Smith, 6, Jim Peaco, 26; Shutterstock: 2009fotofriends, 20, Alexander Sviridov, 15, Christopher May, 14, Danita Delimont, 9, Don Mammoser, 29, Edwin Butter, cover (top left), Geoffrey Kuchera, 21, Holly Kuchera, 13 (left), Krasula, 10, Laura Hedien, cover (top right), Lisa Stoorza, 7, Maciej Olszewski, 12 (bottom), MaLija (background), cover, back cover, and throughout, meunierd, 28, Morphart Creation, 22, N K, cover (bottom), back cover (top), Pablo Garcia Saldana, 13 (right), Pawel Brud, 16–17, Rafal Szozda, 12 (top)

All internet sites appearing in back matter were available and accurate when this book was sent to press.
Printed and bound in the USA. 5425

Table of Contents

Words in **bold** are in the glossary.

CHAPTER ONE

On the Prowl

Night is falling in Yellowstone National Park, a protected stretch of mountains and forest in Idaho, Montana, and Wyoming. As the moon rises over the snowy landscape, an eerie howl breaks the stillness. Then another. A pack of gray wolves is on the hunt. The pack's **prey** is a young bison that wandered away from its herd.

A pack of gray wolves stalks a bison in Yellowstone National Park.

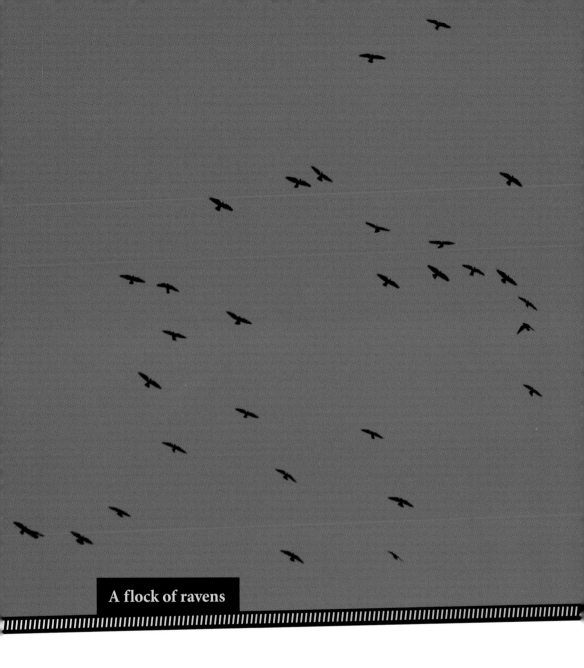

A flock of ravens

The wolves are not alone. The sky above them is filled with a flock of large, black birds—ravens. The ravens follow the hunt through the night.

The young bison is fast. But the wolves are hungry and clever. They surround the bison and chase it for hours. By daybreak, the bison is exhausted. That's when the wolves attack.

They bite the bison on its shoulder and **flank**. The bison falls, and the wolves move in to feed.

A gray wolf and ravens surround the remains of a bison.

Again, they are not alone. As the wolves tear into their meal, the ravens swoop down to pluck morsels of meat from the kill.

DID YOU KNOW?

Wolves can eat as much as 20 pounds (9 kilograms) of meat at one time and then not eat for as many as three days.

CHAPTER TWO

Predator, Scavenger, Partner

The wolf is the largest member of the **canine** family, which also includes dogs, jackals, and coyotes. Layers of brown, black, gray, and white fur coat its body. Long, skinny legs help it move fast over land and bound through snow. Its strong jaws can crush bone. Its large, sharp teeth can tear off chunks of flesh in one bite. The wolf isn't a pure **carnivore**. Besides meat, it eats fruit and plants.

Adult wolves with their pups

Wolves are social animals that live in close-knit packs throughout North America, Europe, and Asia. They mate for life, and "aunts" and "uncles" in the pack help raise the pups.

Wolves growl, bark, and howl to pass information about prey, send warnings, and locate one another during a hunt. When a pack member dies, the remaining wolves show signs of stress.

Ravens are **scavengers**—meaning they eat just about anything they can find, including **carrion**. Large birds with black feathers, beaks, and eyes, they are acrobats in the air. They swoop and dive and even do somersaults.

Ravens communicate with a range of noises, including croaks, gurgles, knocking sounds, and cries of warning. They are also masters at copying the calls of other birds—and can even learn a few words of human speech!

Common ravens

Ravens are curious and very playful. They have been seen sliding down snowy hills and dropping sticks and pine cones to fetch. They've even been known to unzip backpacks to get at the food inside!

A raven attempts to open a backpack in search of food.

At some point in the past, wolves and ravens formed a partnership that benefits them both. This relationship, known as **symbiotic mutualism**, has been recorded so far back in history that scientists think it could be part of their natures now.

Notice the Difference?

Ravens often get confused with crows. Here's how to tell the difference:

▌ Ravens are bigger.

▌ When flying, a raven's tail feathers fan out in a distinct triangular shape. The crow's tail is slightly rounded.

▌ Ravens croak and shriek; crows caw.

RAVEN

CROW

WOLF

COYOTE

Wolves and coyotes look a lot alike, too. But there are differences:

▌ Wolves are bigger. They can weigh as much as 175 pounds (79 kg); coyotes weigh about 50 pounds (23 kg).

▌ The wolf's muzzle is broad and square; a coyote's is long and pointed.

▌ Wolves steer clear of most human habitats; coyotes can be found roaming neighborhoods and cities.

CHAPTER THREE

Partners at Work

Ravens and wolves join together for one simple reason: food. But how does this partnership work? Sounds play a big role. If a raven sitting in a tree or flying over a field spots possible prey, it will alert nearby wolves. Likewise, howling wolves let ravens know that a pack is about to hunt. When the chase is on, both are on the move!

Ravens and wolves help one another find food when not hunting, too. Both species eat carrion. Because ravens can fly, they often see old or recent kills sooner. Sometimes, though, a **carcass** is too old, tough, or frozen for them to rip into with their beaks. That's when they call on their partners.

The wolves will follow ravens in flight to the carcass. Once the wolves have ripped into the remains, the ravens dive in for their share.

A grizzly bear, wolves, and ravens compete for a bison kill.

Animals are most likely to be attacked when they're feeding. But partners ravens and wolves have a lookout system. Ravens use alarm calls to signal incoming danger such as other **predators** ready to challenge the wolves for food. Wolves, meanwhile, keep ravens safe just by being there!

A wolf that has left or been driven out of the pack is called a "lone wolf." Ravens are often associated with bad tidings. That's why a flock is also known as an "unkindness"!

A gray wolf, ravens, and magpies near a bison carcass

DID YOU KNOW?

The close relationship between ravens and wolves has led to a nickname for the ravens: wolf-birds.

CHAPTER FOUR

Partners at Play

Ravens and wolves don't just work together. They play together too! The birds use sticks to play tug-of-war with wolf pups. They also fly over the young wolves with sticks in their beaks to get the pups to jump for the toys. And sometimes, one will swoop down and give a pup's tail a little tug—just to see what the wolf will do!

Gray wolf pups play with each other.

Playtime strengthens relationships between these two very different species. Strong relationships mean better **cooperation** while hunting and scavenging. Better cooperation means more food for both ravens and wolves!

A Legendary Partnership

Raven and wolf partnerships show up in different world **mythologies**.

▌ In Norse mythology, Odin, the All-Father, uses his two ravens (Huginn and Muninn) and his two wolves (Geri and Freki) to teach humans how to cooperate.

▎A Cree creation myth says Raven and Wolf worked together to form land on the flooded Earth.

▎A tattoo that shows both the raven and the wolf symbolizes either wisdom. . . or destruction!

CHAPTER FIVE

A Partnership in Jeopardy

Wolves have very few natural enemies. Bears are one. Humans are another.

Once, hundreds of thousands of wolves roamed throughout the United States. But in the early 1900s, ranchers and farmers began losing livestock to the predators. So, they hunted the wolves. They killed so many that by the 1960s, only a few hundred remained.

Hunters with killed wolves

The ravens lost their partners and the carrion they once shared with the wolves. The birds **adapted** by moving closer to humans and feeding on their crops and garbage. The hungry, noisy ravens turned into agricultural pests—a situation that might not have occurred if people had left their wolf partners alone.

DID YOU KNOW?

In the 1920s, the last remaining wolves in Yellowstone National Park were killed. In 1995, eight wolves were set free in the park. The population has numbered between 8 and 528 ever since.

Wolves became a protected species in the U.S. in 1974. Instead of killing them, people began helping them. Wolves were reintroduced to many of their natural **habitats**. And ravens have migrated away from humans to rejoin their centuries-old partners.

A gray wolf is released into Yellowstone National Park in 1996.

A wolf pack crosses the Lamar Valley in Yellowstone National Park.

DID YOU KNOW?

Scientists, wolf watchers, and bird-watchers tag and track wolves and ravens with electronic devices to study their behavior and log their numbers and locations.

THE WOLF

Also Known As: Gray Wolf, Timber Wolf

Species: *Canis lupus*; family includes dogs, coyotes, and jackals

Size: 28–30 inches (71–76 centimeters) tall at shoulder; 6 feet (1.8 meters) long from nose to tail

Weight: 100–145 pounds (45–66 kg)

Fur: Coarse texture; brown, black, gray, and white

Features: Powerful jaws; small, pointed ears; blunt muzzle; common eye colors are yellow, orange, hazel, light brown, green

Pack Size: 8–12

As a Hunting Ally: Howls to signal the start of a hunt; protects ravens with its presence at a kill

THE RAVEN

Also Known As: Wolf-bird, Common Raven

Species: *Corvus corax*; family includes crows

Size: 21–26 inches (53–66 cm) long; 3.8–4.5 feet (1.1–1.2 m) wingspan

Weight: 1.5–4.5 pounds (0.68–2 kg)

Feathers: Glossy black

Features: Black eyes, black beak, gray to black legs

Flock Size: Varies

As a Hunting Ally: Alerts wolves to the presence of prey, carrion, and when unwelcome predators are near

Glossary

adapt (uh-DAPT)—to adjust due to specific circumstances

canine (KAY-nine)—of or about the dog family, including wolves and coyotes

carcass (KAR-kuhss)—the body of a dead animal

carnivore (KAR-nuh-vor)—an animal that feeds on flesh

carrion (KARE-ee-uhn)—the decaying flesh of a dead animal

cooperation (koh-op-er-AY-shun)—the process of working together to achieve a common goal

flank (FLANGK)— the fleshy part of the side between the ribs and the hip

habitat (HAB-i-tat)—a natural home of an animal or plant

mutualism (MYOO-choo-uhl-ism)—a partnership that benefits both animals involved

mythology (mith-OL-uh-gee)—a collection of stories associated with a culture or religion

predator (PRED-uh-tor)—an animal that naturally preys on other animals

prey (PRAY)—an animal that is hunted and killed by other animals, usually for food

scavenger (SKAV-uhn-jer)—an animal that feeds on carrion, dead plant material, or garbage

symbiotic (sim-by-OT-ik)—involving a close relationship and interaction between two animal species

Read More

Corrigan, Sophie. *Animal BFFs: Even Animals Have Best Friends!* Minneapolis: Frances Lincoln Children's Books, 2022.

Herrington, Lisa M. *Gray Wolves.* New York: Children's Press, 2018.

Lajiness, Katie. *Ravens: Problem Solvers.* Minneapolis: Abdo, 2018.

Internet Sites

The Cornell Lab: All About Birds: Common Raven Sounds
allaboutbirds.org/guide/Common_Raven/sounds

Living with Wolves
livingwithwolves.org

Yellowstone Forever: Naturalist Notes: Wolves and Ravens
yellowstone.org/naturalist-notes-wolves-and-ravens

Index

About the Author

Stephanie Peters has been writing books for young readers for more than 25 years. Among her most recent titles are *Sleeping Beauty: Magic Master* and *Johnny Slimeseed*, both for Capstone's Far-Out Fairy Tales and Folk Tales series. An avid reader, workout enthusiast, and beach wanderer, Stephanie enjoys spending time with her children, Jackson and Chloe, her husband Dan, and the family's two cats and two rabbits. She lives and works in Mansfield, Massachusetts.